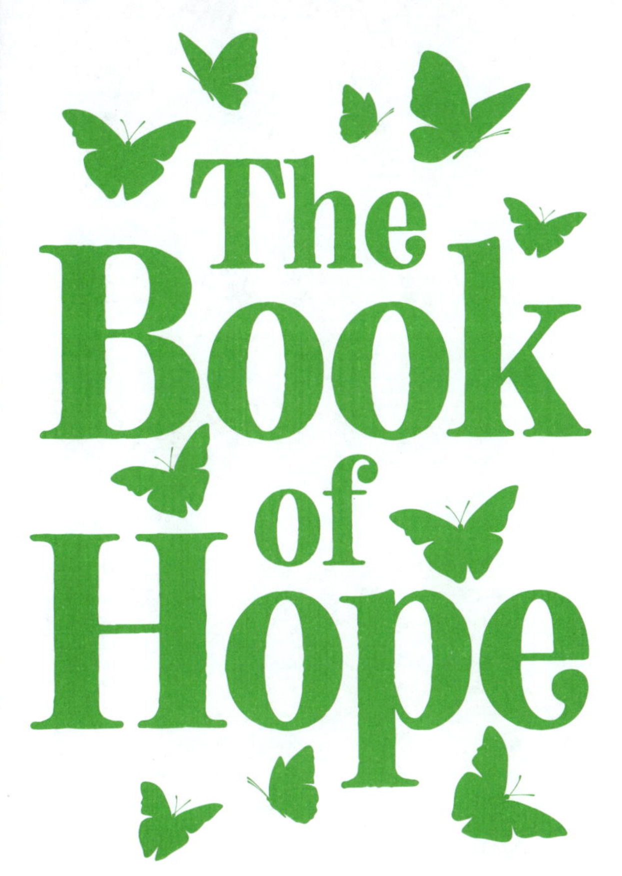
The
Book
of
Hope

Published 2026

FiNGERPRINT!
Prakash Books

Fingerprint Publishing
@FingerprintP
@fingerprintpublishingbooks
www.fingerprintpublishing.com

ISBN: 978 93 5856 218 7

To....................
From..................

Hope is faith in the future.

A belief against all odds that keeps you going. It is an emotion that can rarely be defined but its presence is felt by all.

Contrary to what people believe, hope is not a constant state of mind.

It is a feeling that you have to cultivate every day which ultimately becomes the cornerstone of a happy life.

So, whenever you are going through times when the world seems gloomy and you feel defeated, keep that little ray of hope in your pocket and look for the light at the end of the tunnel!

"MY HOPES ARE NOT ALWAYS REALIZED, BUT I ALWAYS HOPE."

Ovid

"We need never be hopeless because we can never be irreparably broken."

ALBERT EINSTEIN

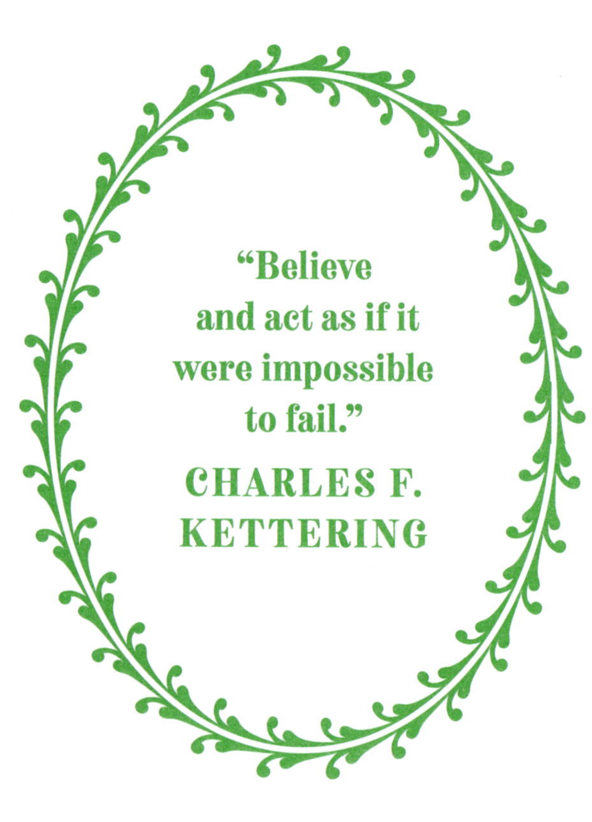

"Believe
and act as if it
were impossible
to fail."

CHARLES F.
KETTERING

"To love means loving the unlovable. To forgive means pardoning the unpardonable. Faith means believing the unbelievable. Hope means hoping when everything seems hopeless."

G.K. CHESTERTON

“Rules for Happiness:
something to do,
someone to love,
something to hope for.”

**IMMANUEL
KANT**

"As far as you can avoid it, do not give grief to anyone. Never inflict your rage on another. If you hope for eternal rest, feel the pain yourself; but don't hurt others."

OMAR KHAYYAM

"For what it's worth, it's never too late to be whoever you want to be. I hope you live a life you're proud of and if you find that you're not, I hope you have the strength to start over."

F. SCOTT FITZGERALD

"To love is to risk not being loved in return. To hope is to risk pain. To try is to risk failure, but risk must be taken because the greatest hazard in my life is to risk nothing."

BOB MARLEY

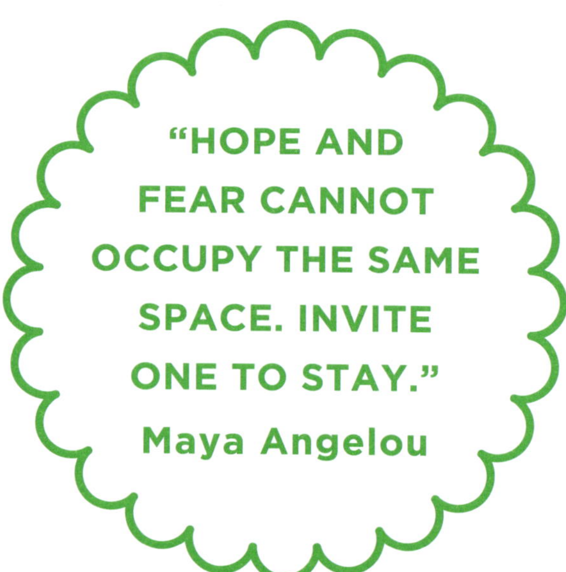
"HOPE AND
FEAR CANNOT
OCCUPY THE SAME
SPACE. INVITE
ONE TO STAY."
Maya Angelou

"Hope has two beautiful daughters; their names are Anger and Courage. Anger at the way things are, and Courage to see that they do not remain as they are."

SAINT AUGUSTINE

"OPTIMISM IS THE FAITH THAT LEADS TO ACHIEVEMENT. NOTHING CAN BE DONE WITHOUT HOPE AND CONFIDENCE."

Helen Keller

"PROMISES ARE WORSE THAN LIES. YOU DON'T JUST MAKE THEM BELIEVE, YOU ALSO MAKE THEM HOPE."

Marilyn Monroe

"Hope is the thing that keeps you going when the odds are against you."

JOHN C. MAXWELL

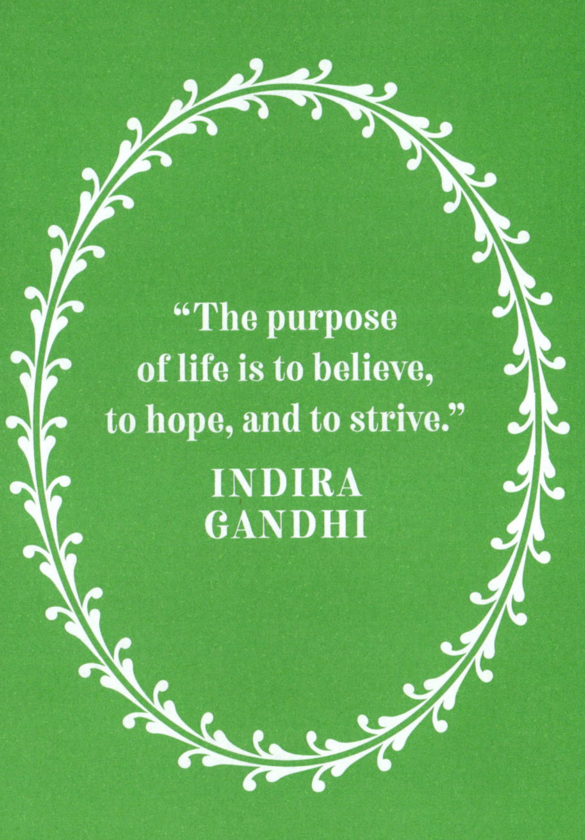

"The purpose
of life is to believe,
to hope, and to strive."

INDIRA
GANDHI

"Don't be sad! Because God sends hope in the most desperate moments. Don't forget, the heaviest rain comes out of the darkest clouds."

RUMI

"Somewhere over the rainbow, skies are blue, and the dreams that you dare to dream really do come true."

JUDY GARLAND

“HOPE IS SWEET.
HOPE IS ILLUMINATING.
HOPE IS FULFILLING
HOPE CAN BE EVERLASTING.
THEREFORE, DO NOT GIVE
UP HOPE, EVEN IN THE
SUNSET OF YOUR LIFE.”

Sri Chinmoy

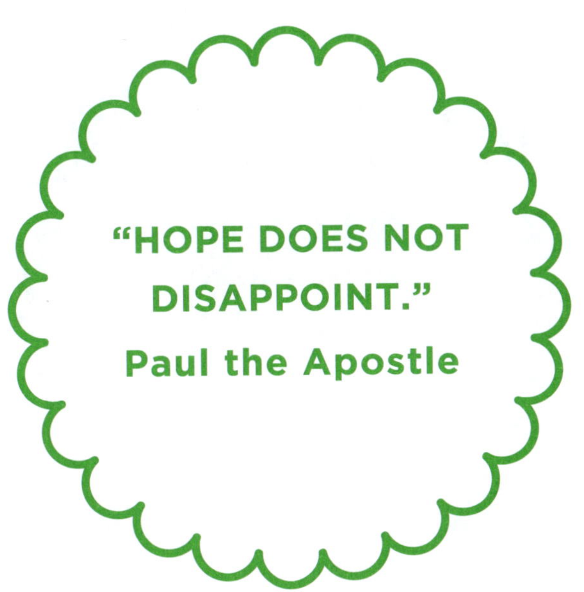
"HOPE DOES NOT
DISAPPOINT."
Paul the Apostle

"The child is both hope and a promise for mankind."

MARIA MONTESSORI

"Be faithful in small things because it is in them that your strength lies."

MOTHER TERESA

"It's really a wonder that I haven't dropped all my ideals, because they seem so absurd and impossible to carry out. Yet I keep them, because in spite of everything, I still believe that people are really good at heart."

ANNE FRANK

"Hope lies in dreams,
in imagination, and in the
courage of those who dare
to make dreams into reality."

JONAS SALK

"Hope is the thing with feathers that perches in the soul and sings the tune without the words and never stops at all."

EMILY DICKINSON

"Love is a springtime plant that perfumes everything with its hope, even the ruins to which it clings."

GUSTAVE FLAUBERT

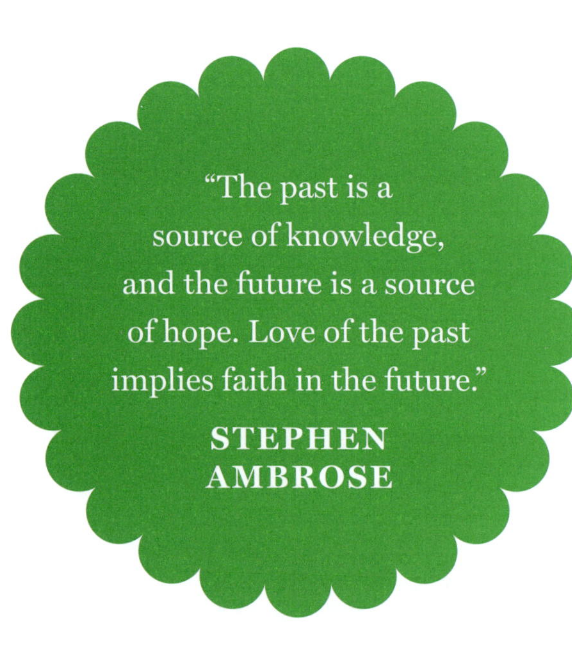
"The past is a
source of knowledge,
and the future is a source
of hope. Love of the past
implies faith in the future."
STEPHEN
AMBROSE

"WE HAVE ALWAYS HELD TO THE HOPE, THE BELIEF, THE CONVICTION THAT THERE IS A BETTER LIFE, A BETTER WORLD, BEYOND THE HORIZON."

Franklin D. Roosevelt

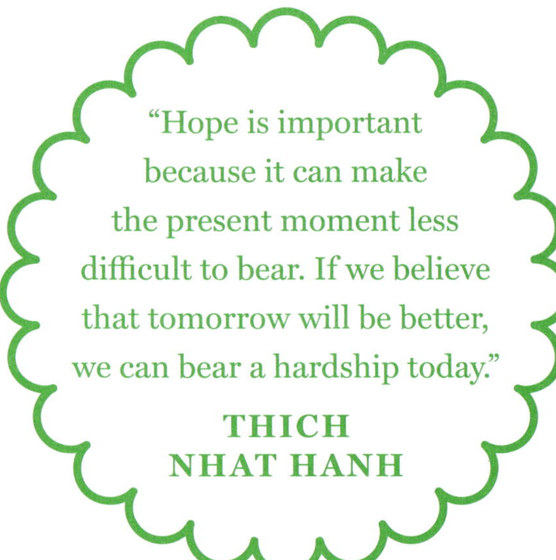
"Hope is important
because it can make
the present moment less
difficult to bear. If we believe
that tomorrow will be better,
we can bear a hardship today."
THICH
NHAT HANH

"Our human compassion binds the one to the other—not in pity or patronizingly, but as human beings who have learned how to turn our common suffering into hope for the future."

NELSON MANDELA

"HOPE SMILES FROM THE THRESHOLD OF THE YEAR TO COME, WHISPERING 'IT WILL BE HAPPIER' . . ."

Alfred Lord Tennyson

"IN FACT, HOPE IS BEST GAINED AFTER DEFEAT AND FAILURE, BECAUSE THEN INNER STRENGTH AND TOUGHNESS IS PRODUCED."

Fritz Knapp

"A positive statement propels
hope toward a better future,
it builds up your faith and that of
others, and it promotes change."

JAN DARGATZ

"You are not here merely to make
a living, you are here in order
to enable the world to live more
amply, with greater vision,
with a finer spirit of hope and
achievement. You are here to enrich
the world, and you impoverish
yourself if you forget the errand."

WOODROW WILSON

"IT'S ALWAYS SOMETHING, TO KNOW YOU'VE DONE THE MOST YOU COULD. BUT, DON'T LEAVE OFF HOPING, OR IT'S OF NO USE DOING ANYTHING. HOPE, HOPE TO THE LAST."

Charles Dickens

"We must accept finite disappointment, but never lose infinite hope."

MARTIN LUTHER KING JR.

"WE MUST VOTE FOR HOPE, VOTE FOR LIFE, VOTE FOR A BRIGHTER FUTURE FOR ALL OF OUR LOVED ONES."

Ed Markey

"HOPE IS THE COMPANION OF POWER, AND MOTHER OF SUCCESS; FOR WHO SO HOPES STRONGLY HAS WITHIN HIM THE GIFT OF MIRACLES."

Samuel Smiles

"A dream is
the bearer of a
new possibility, the
enlarged horizon,
the great hope."

**HOWARD
THURMAN**

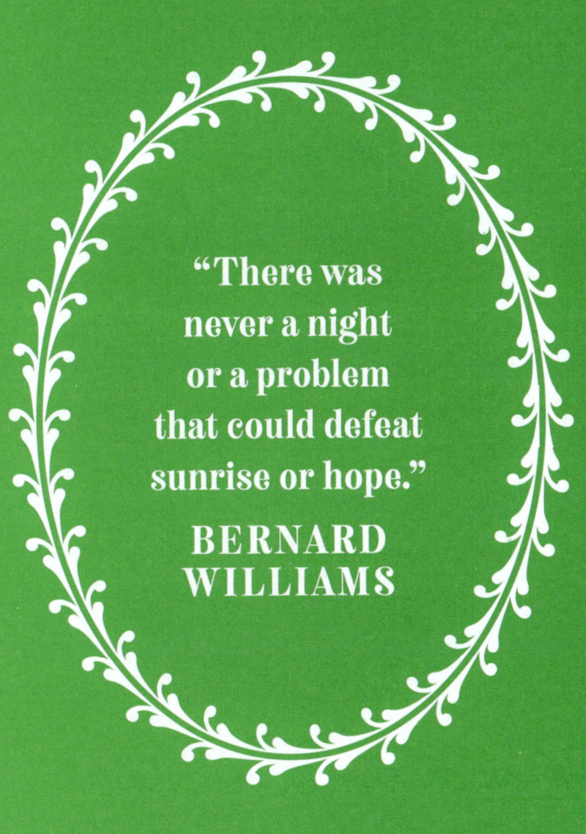

“There was never a night or a problem that could defeat sunrise or hope.”

BERNARD WILLIAMS

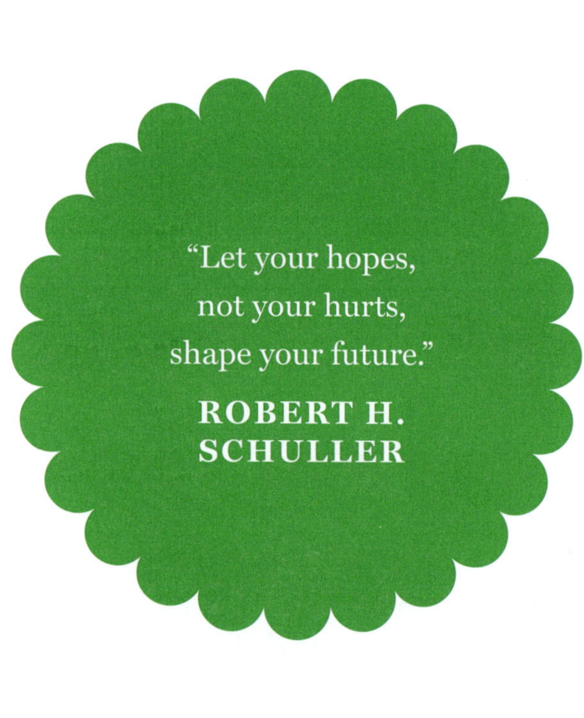
"Let your hopes,
not your hurts,
shape your future."
ROBERT H.
SCHULLER

"HOPE IS THE WHISPER OF OUR HEART."

Anonymous

WHY YOU SHOULD BE HOPEFUL?

- Being hopeful keeps you optimistic and helps you manage your stress and anxiety.
- It boosts your self-esteem and allows you to thrive in both your personal and professional life!
- Hope keeps you happy and healthy, which has proven to increase one's life expectancy.
- Being hopeful about the future encourages you to explore new possibilities.
- Hope makes you an empathetic person and develops your critical thinking abilities!

“To live without hope is to cease to live.”

FYODOR DOSTOEVSKY

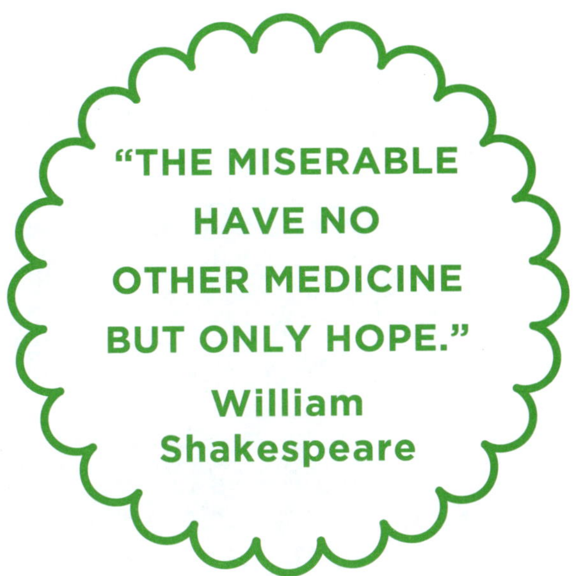
"THE MISERABLE
HAVE NO
OTHER MEDICINE
BUT ONLY HOPE."
William
Shakespeare

"I THINK IT'S A MISTAKE TO EVER LOOK FOR HOPE OUTSIDE OF ONE'S SELF."

Arthur Miller

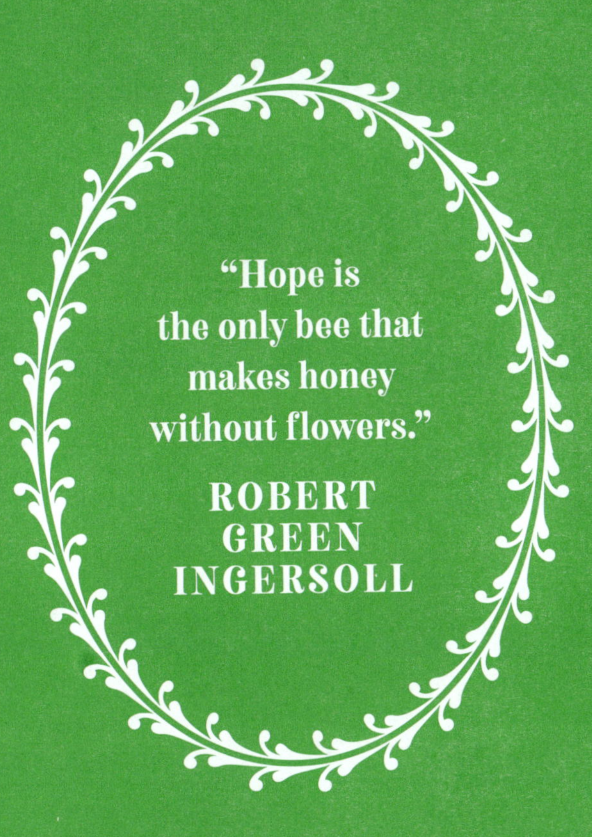

“Hope is
the only bee that
makes honey
without flowers.”

ROBERT
GREEN
INGERSOLL

"A whole stack
of memories never
equal one little hope."

CHARLES M. SCHULZ

"He who has health,
has hope; and he
who has hope
has everything."

**THOMAS
CARLYLE**

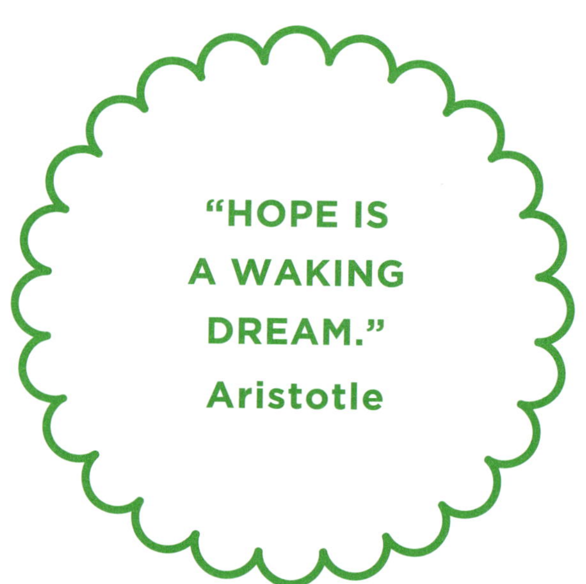
"HOPE IS
A WAKING
DREAM."
Aristotle

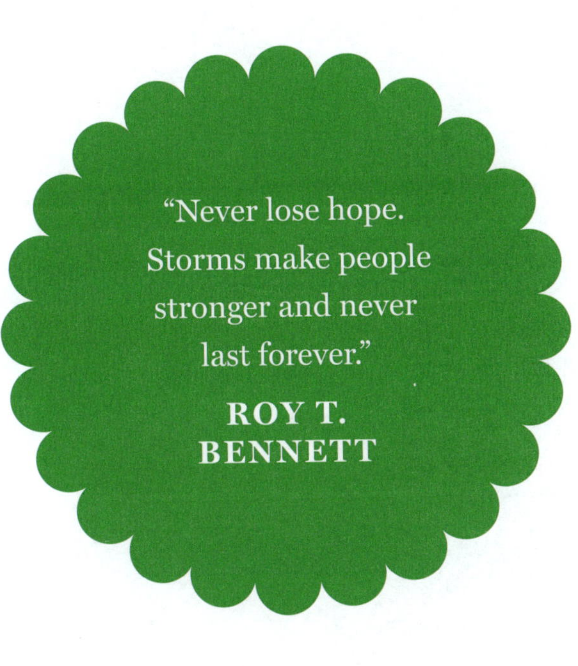
"Never lose hope.
Storms make people
stronger and never
last forever."
ROY T.
BENNETT

"You are never too old to set another goal or to dream a new dream."

C.S. LEWIS

"There is some good in this world,
and it's worth fighting for."

J.R.R. TOLKIEN

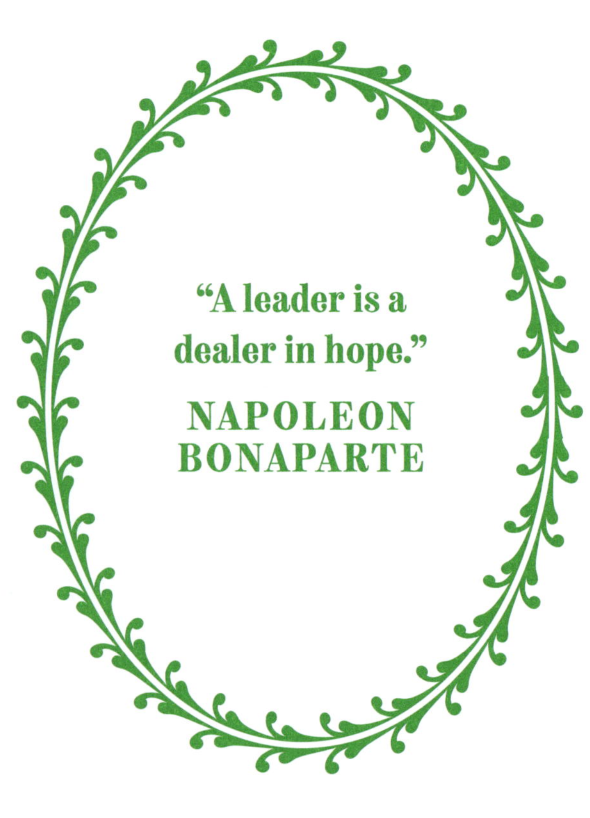
“A leader is a
dealer in hope.”
NAPOLEON
BONAPARTE

“DO NOT SPOIL WHAT YOU HAVE BY DESIRING WHAT YOU HAVE NOT; REMEMBER THAT WHAT YOU NOW HAVE WAS ONCE AMONG THE THINGS YOU ONLY HOPED FOR.”

Epicurus

“Hope is a renewable option:
If you run out of it at the end
of the day, you get to start
over in the morning.”

BARBARA KINGSOLVER

"Learn to ask even when you feel weak.
Learn to work even if you don't want to.
Learn to hope even when the odds
are against you."

MAXIME LAGACÉ

"Hope is like a road
in the country;
there was never a road,
but when many
people walk on it,
the road comes
into existence."

LIN YUTANG

"There is no medicine like hope, no incentive so great, and no tonic so powerful as expectation of something tomorrow."

O. S. MARDEN

"YOU ARE FULL OF UNSHAPED DREAMS . . . YOU ARE LADEN WITH BEGINNINGS . . . THERE IS HOPE IN YOU . . ."

Lola Ridge

“THE FUTURE BELONGS TO THOSE WHO BELIEVE IN THE BEAUTY OF THEIR DREAMS.”

Eleanor Roosevelt

“I AM PREPARED
FOR THE WORST, BUT
HOPE FOR THE BEST.”

Benjamin Disraeli

"A STRONG MIND ALWAYS HOPES, AND HAS ALWAYS CAUSE TO HOPE."

Thomas Carlyle

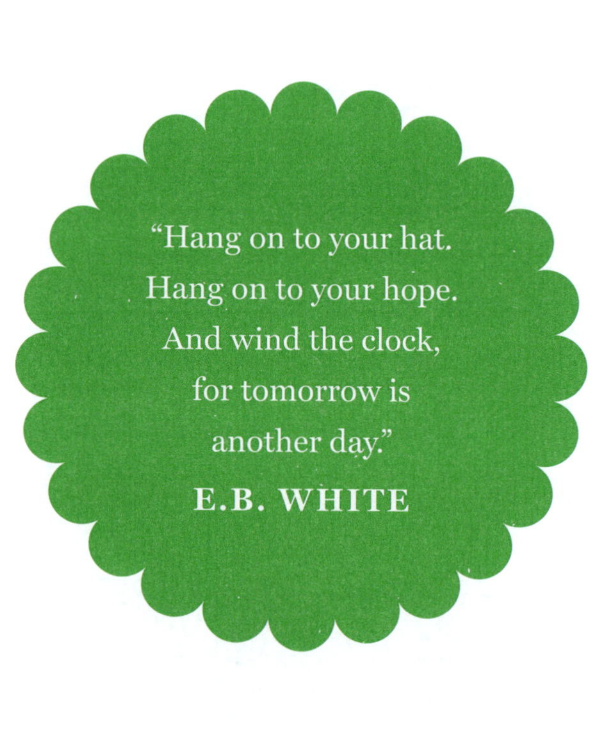
"Hang on to your hat.
Hang on to your hope.
And wind the clock,
for tomorrow is
another day."
E.B. WHITE

"As long as we have hope,
we have direction,
the energy to move,
and the map to move by."

LAO TZU

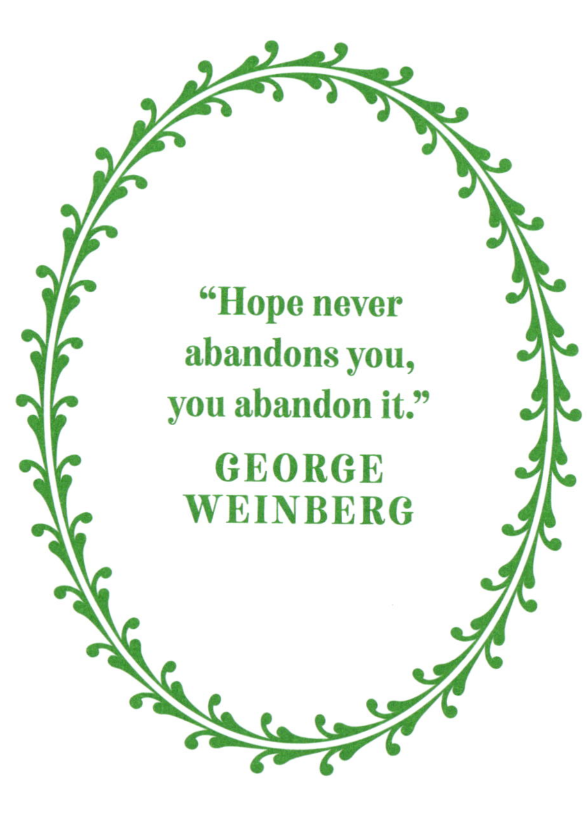

"Hope never abandons you, you abandon it."

GEORGE WEINBERG

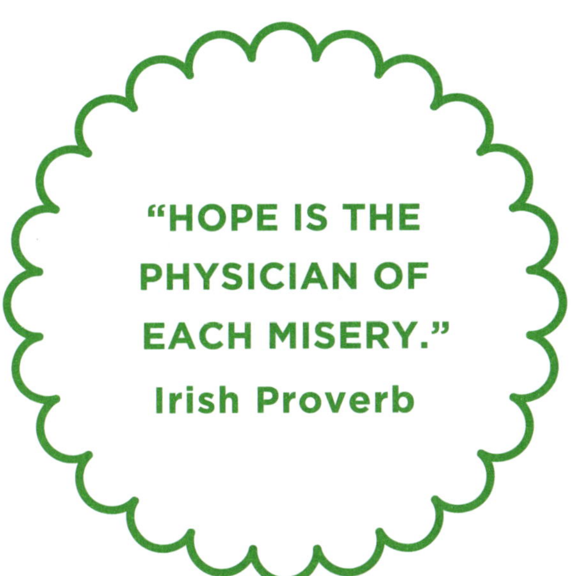
"HOPE IS THE
PHYSICIAN OF
EACH MISERY."
Irish Proverb

"Many of life's failures are people who did not realize how close they were to success when they gave up."

THOMAS EDISON

“To wish was to hope,
and to hope was to expect.”

JANE AUSTEN

"THE BEST BRIDGE BETWEEN DESPAIR AND HOPE IS A GOOD NIGHT'S SLEEP."

E. Joseph Cossman

"Once you choose hope, anything's possible."

CHRISTOPHER REEVE

"For every dark night there's a brighter day."

TUPAC

"Hope is the word which God has written on the brow of every man."

VICTOR HUGO

“HOPE IS THE WHISPER THAT REMINDS US TO KEEP GOING WHEN EVERYTHING SEEMS TO BE FALLING APART.”

Anonymous

"Hope has bred change again and again."

AVA DUVERNAY

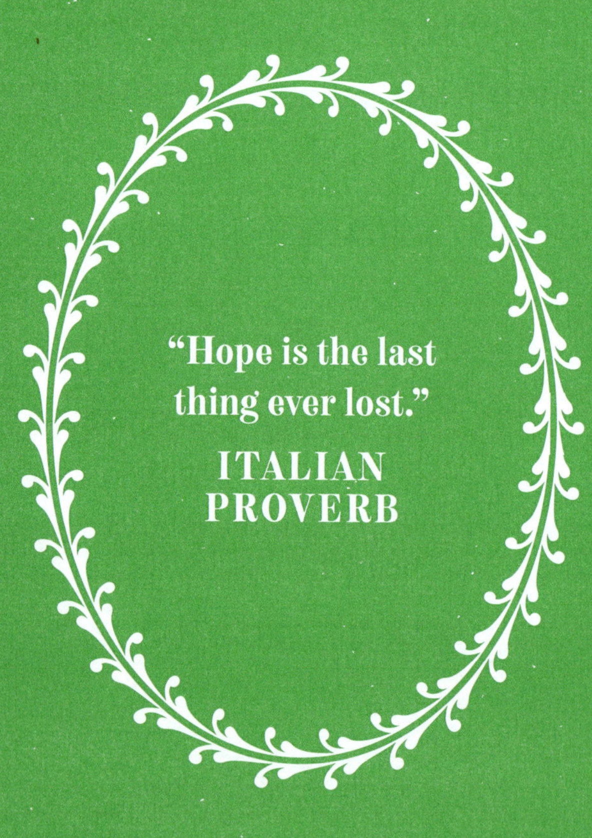
“Hope is the last thing ever lost.”
ITALIAN PROVERB

"The basis for hope
is to have a sense
of brotherhood and
sisterhood, mindful of
the oneness of all seven
billion human beings."

14TH DALAI LAMA

"If you have
a wounded heart,
touch it as little as you
would an injured eye.
There are only two
remedies for the
suffering of the soul:
hope and patience."

PYTHAGORAS

“Hope is not a matter of waiting for things outside of us to get better. It is about getting better inside about what is going on outside.”

JOAN D. CHITTISTER

"Carve a tunnel of hope
through the dark mountain
of disappointment."

MARTIN LUTHER KING JR.

"We promise according to our hopes and perform according to our fears."

FRANÇOIS DE LA ROCHEFOUCAULD

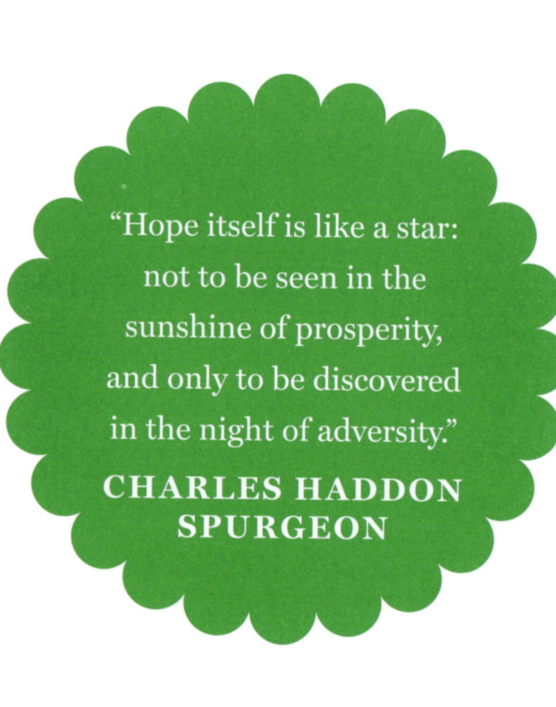
"Hope itself is like a star:
not to be seen in the
sunshine of prosperity,
and only to be discovered
in the night of adversity."
CHARLES HADDON
SPURGEON

“HOPE IS NOT AN EMOTION; IT’S A WAY OF THINKING OR A COGNITIVE PROCESS.”

Brené Brown

"HE WHO HAS NEVER HOPED CAN NEVER DESPAIR."

George Bernard Shaw

"HOPE SEES THE INVISIBLE,
FEELS THE INTANGIBLE, AND
ACHIEVES THE IMPOSSIBLE."

Helen Keller

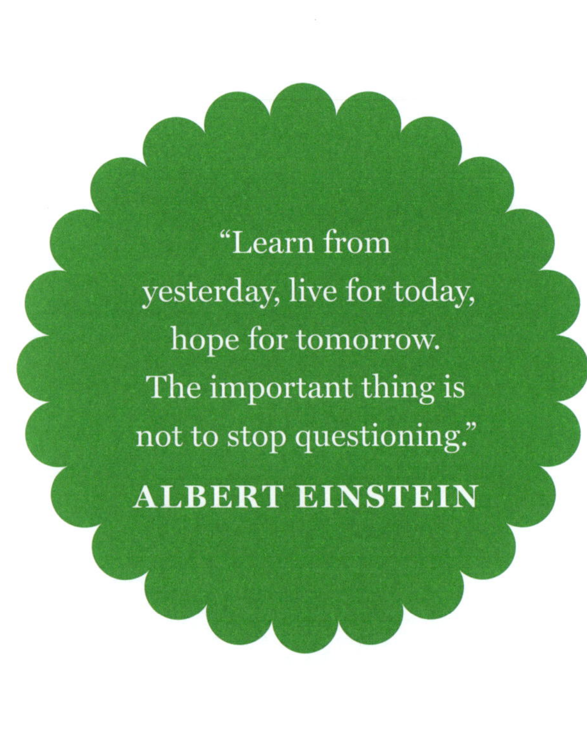
"Learn from
yesterday, live for today,
hope for tomorrow.
The important thing is
not to stop questioning."
ALBERT EINSTEIN

"Live, then, and be happy, beloved children of my heart, and never forget, that until the day God will deign to reveal the future to man, all human wisdom is contained in these two words, Wait and Hope."

ALEXANDRE DUMAS

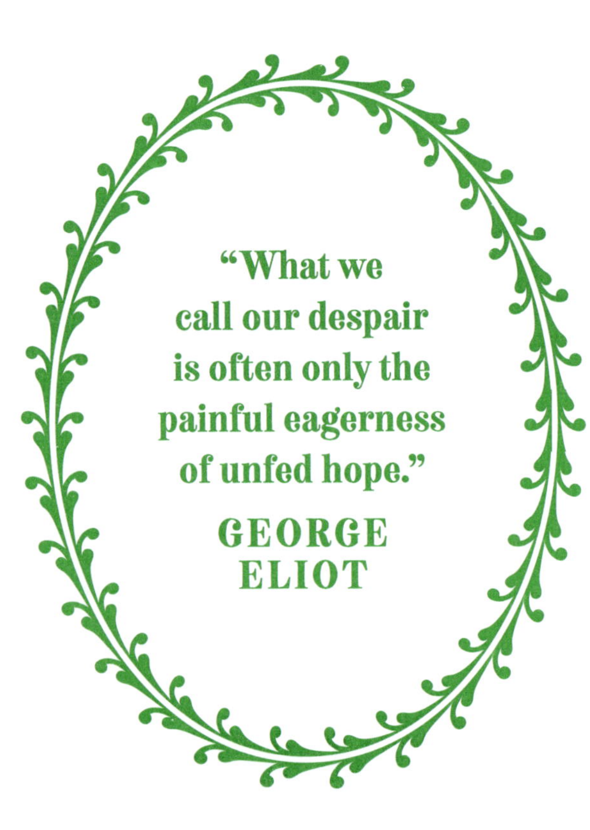
"What we
call our despair
is often only the
painful eagerness
of unfed hope."
GEORGE
ELIOT

"WHEN YOU FEEL LIKE HOPE IS GONE, LOOK INSIDE YOU AND BE STRONG AND YOU'LL FINALLY SEE THE TRUTH— THAT HERO LIES IN YOU."

Mariah Carey

"All the great things are simple, and many can be expressed in a single word: freedom, justice, honor, duty, mercy, hope."

WINSTON CHURCHILL

"In joined hands there is still some token of hope, in the clinched fist, none."

VICTOR HUGO

"HOPE IS THE MOST EXCITING THING IN LIFE AND IF YOU HONESTLY BELIEVE THAT LOVE IS OUT THERE, IT WILL COME. AND EVEN IF IT DOESN'T COME STRAIGHT AWAY THERE IS STILL THAT CHANCE ALL THROUGH YOUR LIFE THAT IT WILL."

Josh Hartnett

"A LITTLE MORE PERSISTENCE, A LITTLE MORE EFFORT, AND WHAT SEEMED HOPELESS FAILURE MAY TURN TO GLORIOUS SUCCESS."

Elbert Hubbard

"Never deprive someone of hope;
it might be all they have."

H. JACKSON BROWN, JR.

"Hope is a passion
for the infinite possibilities."

SØREN KIERKEGAARD

“The human heart has hidden treasures— In secret kept, in silence sealed; The thoughts, the hopes, the dreams, the pleasures, Whose charms were broken if revealed.”

CHARLOTTE BRONTE

"Just as despair can come to one only from other human beings, hope, too, can be given to one only by other human beings."

ELIE WIESEL

"Most of the important things in the world have been accomplished by people who have kept on trying when there seemed to be no hope at all."

DALE CARNEGIE

"This new day is too dear, with its hopes and invitations, to waste a moment on yesterdays."

RALPH WALDO EMERSON

HOPE ITSELF IS A SPECIES OF HAPPINESS, AND, PERHAPS, THE CHIEF HAPPINESS WHICH THIS WORLD AFFORDS; BUT, LIKE ALL OTHER PLEASURES IMMODERATELY ENJOYED, THE EXCESSES OF HOPE MUST BE EXPIATED BY PAIN."

Samuel Johnson

“Hope is the only universal liar who never loses his reputation for veracity.”

ROBERT GREEN INGERSOLL

HOW TO BE HOPEFUL?

- Identify negative thoughts, accept them, but refashion them—it's all about the perspective!
- Accept that some things are out of your control. Redirect your energy to the things that you can actually control.
- Always think of new possibilities! One failed plan or venture does not define your worth. Be resilient in the face of adversity.
- Have a self-care routine! Do whatever brings you happiness.
- Have a support system! Hope thrives in an affectionate environment. So, keep your family and friends close.

"Little progress can be made by merely attempting to repress what is evil. Our great hope lies in developing what is good."

CALVIN COOLIDGE

"When we have
lost everything,
including hope,
life becomes a disgrace,
and death a duty."

W. C. FIELDS

"I SAID
TO MY SOUL,
BE STILL, AND
WAIT WITHOUT HOPE,
FOR HOPE WOULD
BE HOPE FOR THE
WRONG THING."

T. S. Eliot

“Hope is the light that will guide you home.”

ANONYMOUS

“Anyone who doesn’t believe in miracles is not a realist.”

DAVID BEN-GURION

"The work goes on,
the cause endures, the
hope still lives and the
dreams shall never die."

EDWARD KENNEDY

“Hope
will never
be silent.”

HARVEY
MILK

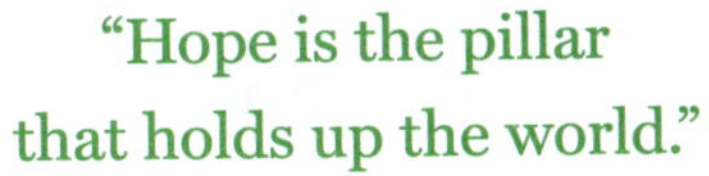

PLINY THE ELDER

"Hope is definitely not
the same thing as optimism.
It is not the conviction that
something will turn out well,
but the certainty that something
makes sense, regardless
of how it turns out."

VACLAV HAVEL

"HOWEVER BAD LIFE MAY SEEM, THERE IS ALWAYS SOMETHING YOU CAN DO AND SUCCEED AT. WHERE THERE'S LIFE, THERE'S HOPE."

Stephen Hawking

"Faith goes up the stairs that love has built and looks out the windows which hope has opened."

CHARLES HADDON SPURGEON

"You can cut
all the flowers but
you cannot keep
Spring from coming."

PABLO NERUDA

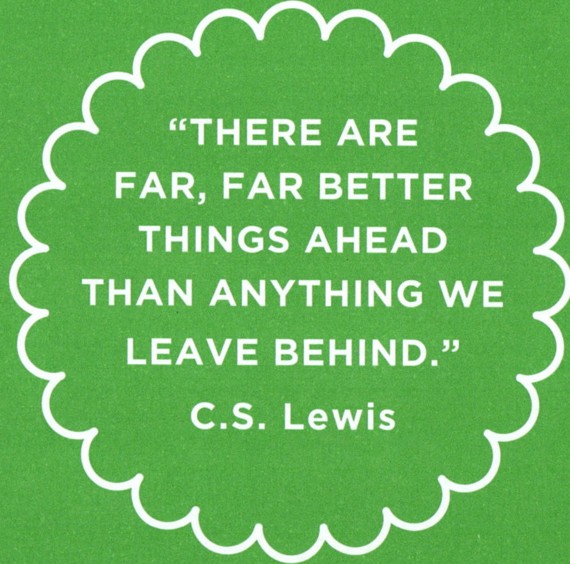
"THERE ARE
FAR, FAR BETTER
THINGS AHEAD
THAN ANYTHING WE
LEAVE BEHIND."
C.S. Lewis

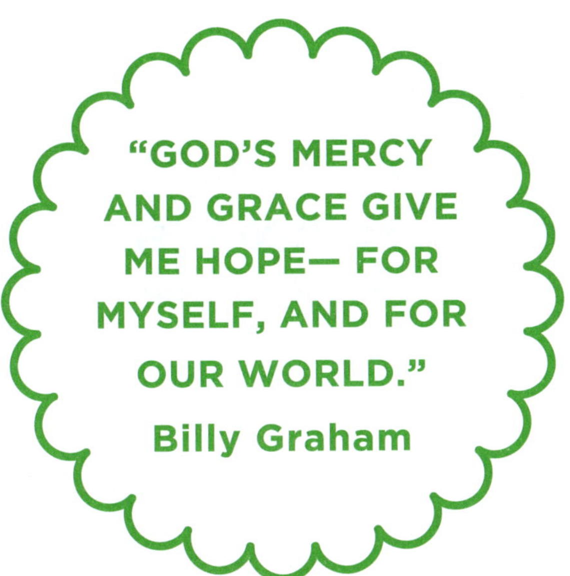

"GOD'S MERCY AND GRACE GIVE ME HOPE— FOR MYSELF, AND FOR OUR WORLD."

Billy Graham

"THERE IS NO HOPE UNMINGLED WITH FEAR, AND NO FEAR UNMINGLED WITH HOPE."

Baruch Spinoza

"Oft hope
is born
when all
is forlorn."
J.R.R.
TOLKIEN

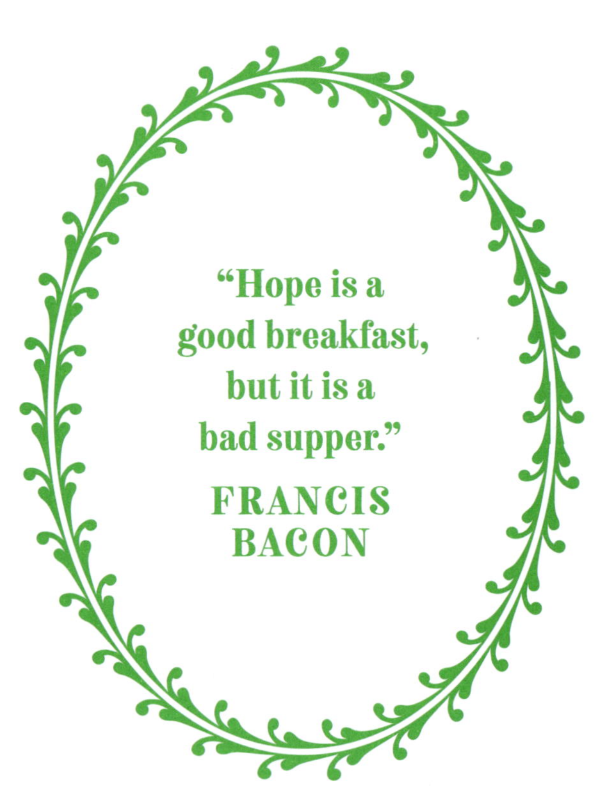
"Hope is a
good breakfast,
but it is a
bad supper."
FRANCIS
BACON

"HOPE AROUSES, AS NOTHING ELSE CAN AROUSE, A PASSION FOR THE POSSIBLE."

WILLIAM SLOANE COFFIN

"Love recognizes
no barriers. It jumps
hurdles, leaps fences,
penetrates walls to
arrive at its destination
full of hope."

MAYA ANGELOU

"Courage is like love;
it must have hope
for nourishment."

NAPOLEON BONAPARTE

"Few things in the world are more powerful than a positive push. A smile. A world of optimism and hope. A 'you can do it' when things are tough."

RICHARD M. DEVOS

“Listen to the mustn’ts, child.
Listen to the don’ts. Listen to the
shouldn’ts, the impossibles, the
won’ts. Listen to the never haves,
then listen close to me . . . Anything
can happen, child. Anything can be.”

SHEL SILVERSTEIN

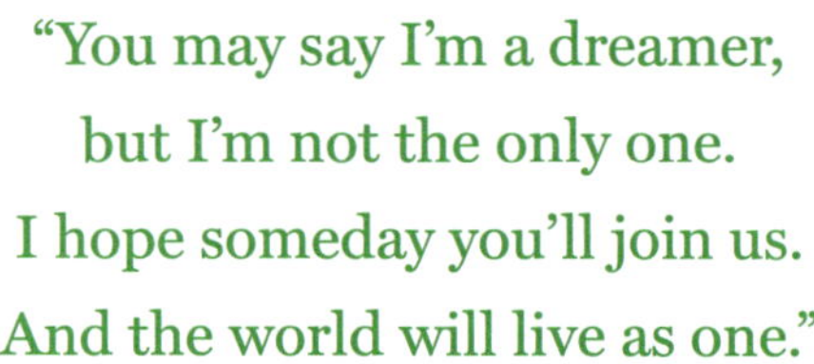
"You may say I'm a dreamer,
but I'm not the only one.
I hope someday you'll join us.
And the world will live as one."

JOHN LENNON

"IT'S AMAZING HOW
A LITTLE TOMORROW CAN
MAKE UP FOR A WHOLE
LOT OF YESTERDAY."

JOHN GUARE

"In a time of destruction, create something."

MAXINE HONG KINGSTON

"When you reach
the end of your rope,
tie a knot in it
and hang on."

**FRANKLIN D.
ROOSEVELT**

“THERE ARE NO HOPELESS SITUATIONS; THERE ARE ONLY PEOPLE WHO HAVE GROWN HOPELESS ABOUT THEM.”

Clare Boothe Luce

“DO NOT GET LOST IN A SEA OF DESPAIR. BE HOPEFUL, BE OPTIMISTIC. OUR STRUGGLE IS NOT THE STRUGGLE OF A DAY, A WEEK, A MONTH, OR A YEAR, IT IS THE STRUGGLE OF A LIFETIME. NEVER, EVER BE AFRAID TO MAKE SOME NOISE AND GET IN GOOD TROUBLE, NECESSARY TROUBLE.”

John Lewis

"A cynic is a man who knows
the price of everything,
and the value of nothing."

OSCAR WILDE

"You cannot swim for new horizons until you have courage to lose sight of the shore."

WILLIAM FAULKNER

"When I despair, I remember that
all through history the way of
truth and love have always won.
There have been tyrants
and murderers, and for a time,
they can seem invincible,
but in the end, they always fall.
Think of it—always."

MAHATMA GANDHI

"In three words I can sum up everything I've learned about life: it goes on."

ROBERT FROST

"When you get into a tight place and everything goes against you . . . never give up then, for that is just the place and time that the tide will turn."

HARRIET BEECHER STOWE

"The world needs less
heat and more light.
It needs less of the
heat of anger, revenge,
retaliation, and more of
the light of ideas, faith,
courage, aspiration,
joy, love and hope."

WILFRED PETERSON

"Every cloud
has a
silver lining."

JOHN
MILSON

“In the midst of winter,
I found there was, within me,
an invincible summer.”

ALBERT CAMUS

"REGARDLESS
OF YOUR PAST,
YOUR FUTURE IS
A CLEAN SLATE."
Anonymous

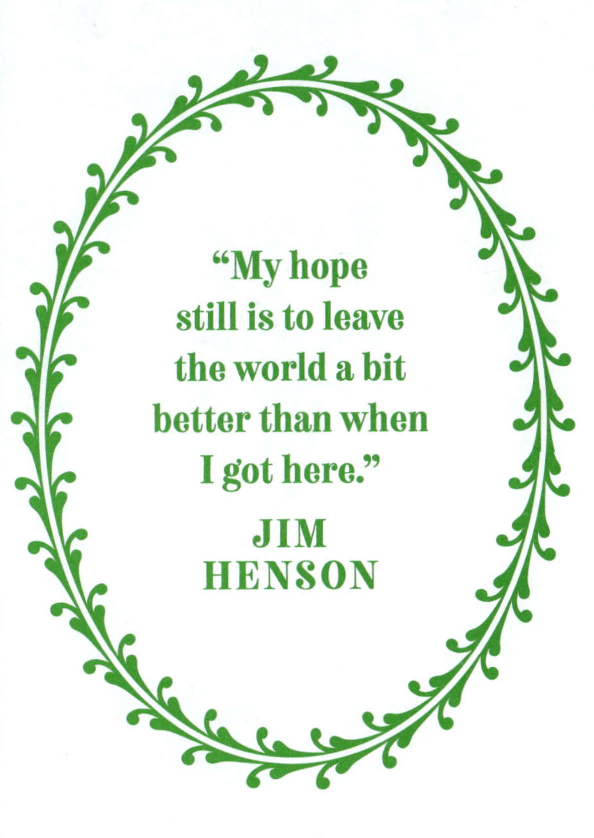

"My hope
still is to leave
the world a bit
better than when
I got here."

**JIM
HENSON**

“Hope is the only thing stronger than fear.”

SUZANNE COLLINS

"HOPE IS THE HAND THAT REACHES THROUGH THE DARKNESS AND PULLS US INTO THE LIGHT."

ANONYMOUS

"HOPE IS THE HEARTBEAT OF THE SOUL."

MICHELLE HORST

"HOPE IS THE
ABILITY TO HEAR
THE MUSIC OF THE
FUTURE; FAITH IS THE
COURAGE TO DANCE
TO IT TODAY."

Peter Kuzmic

"Hope is the power of being cheerful in circumstances that we know to be desperate."

G.K. CHESTERTON

"Where there is no vision, there is no hope."

GEORGE WASHINGTON CARVER

"The darkest hour has only sixty minutes."

MORRIS MANDEL

“What we think,
we become.”

BUDDHA

"I ALWAYS
ENTERTAIN
GREAT HOPES."
Robert Frost